ALL YOUR TALK

Cheryl Follon was born in 1978 in Ayrshire, where she grew up. She studied at the University of Glasgow for four years, switching from Law to English and Scottish Literature, then took an MPhil in Creative Writing at Trinity College Dublin. She now lives in Glasgow. In 2002 she published a pamphlet, *Tales from a Small Island*, with Akros, and was awarded a Scottish Arts Council Writer's Bursary. *All Your Talk* (Bloodaxe Books, 2004) is her first book of poems.

CHERYL FOLLON

All Your Talk

BLOODAXE BOOKS

ISBN: 1 85224 658 8

First published 2004 by
Bloodaxe Books Ltd,
Highgreen,
Tarset,
Northumberland NE48 1RP.

www.bloodaxebooks.com
For further information about Bloodaxe titles
please visit our website or write to
the above address for a catalogue.

Bloodaxe Books Ltd acknowledges
the financial assistance of
Arts Council England, North East.

Cover printing by J. Thomson Colour Printers Ltd, Glasgow.

Printed in Great Britain by
Cromwell Press Ltd, Trowbridge, Wiltshire.

Acknowledgements

My thanks are due to the Scottish Arts Council for a Writer's Bursary awarded in 2002 to help me complete this collection, and to Brendan Kennelly, Gerald Dawe and Harry Clifton at the Oscar Wilde Centre, Trinity College Dublin.

Two poems are reprinted from a Ravenscraig poetry pamphlet, *Tales from a small island* (Akros, 2002). 'Madam Aphrodisia' won third prize in Ireland's Strokestown Poetry Competition in 2002. Some of these poems were first published in *The Dark Horse*, *Northwords* and *The Wolf*.

The cover picture 'Frocking-up Time at the Bordello' (2003) by Priscilla Day (Priscilla Eckhard) was commissioned from Daybreak Productions (specialising in painting on metal objects).

THE SCOTTISH ARTS COUNCIL

Contents

*I kept myself from going mad
by singing an old bawdy ballad*

BASIL BUNTING
'Villon'

Boasts

Fabulla, all your talk wears me down.
In fact I feel quite stripped.
This isn't a contest of strength,
flexing your muscles or violence.
Take a lesson from the girl I love,
how my girl just *peels* my heart.

Sure, you pushed a path through the maul –
all those heavy love songs,
three dozen dancers' demands.
Sure, you came away from that fight
mopping your brow with some flirt's shirt,
while my girl just *teases* her man to the floor.

Sure, every hot-hearted available lover
wants to take you to dinner. I wonder.
And all the no-go ones as well
(that's what comes with being beautiful –
you've made that all quite clear)
while my girl *lulls* over a glass of beer.

Sure, I've heard of your legendary caresses –
heavy hands on a heavier carcass –
a fox that's slipped amongst the sheep
and wants to eat.
No, no Fabulla, look to my girl –
how she *cajoles* the shirt from off my back.

Sure, who am I to say you're telling a lie? –
all the big boasts and endless brags
concerning the hundred and one lovers
you *so* love to give us.
Fabulla, it's a pity you've got no brain,
where my girl just *coaxes* a man to learn.

Upstairs at the Red Hole Tavern

Famous for its women who flavour their cunts
    with sweet-smelling flowers –
        ox-eye daisies,
        wood anemones,
    meadowsweet and stinking clover,
buds of sweet chestnut pulled thick from the branch.

Over the door a bunch of cow parsley
    hunts down bad customers.
    Over each bed
        a crown of black beads
    and bellflowers praise all lovers,
wishing them nights of playful plenty.

Mary-Jane insists on telling lovers
    of other lovers and how they kiss,
        of those who love to bite
        or slap and scream and fight!
    It doesn't matter who she's with –
she'll concoct a story and he'll believe her.

No girl's more infamous than Caitlin –
    raven hair resting on her shoulders,
        a thick silver band
        around each upper arm
    and rings on every finger –
a famous lady of an infamous harem!

Carmel's thighs are looped with a tumble
    of long-flowing crêpe and lace,
        Indian silk and chiffon.
    She puts a record on
    and rhythmically her body shakes
to the little tune and the needle trembles.

Heather mixes a teaspoonful of honey
    with milk from gentle roots –
        a mixture that's slightly oily –
        and spreads it over her belly,
    neck, legs, arms and tits,
then robes herself with a gossamer nightie.

No less than one hundred colours
    have been glimpsed in Annie's hair
        when it's down her back
        and brushed out flat.
    Other women can't be like her.
No – not for a world of beauty parlours.

Willa's hands are like two little doves
    cooing and caressing and playing,
        fluttering their wings
        softly on men's skin
    which is endlessly delighting!
There's no lighter thing than Willa's love.

You can be sure that on this very night
    Katie's pressed beneath a man
        and a soiled sheet.
    Her breathing's quick and short
    and sweat's upon her brow again,
but her eyes sparkle with the sea's light.

Little Janet can't help singing
    snatches of old songs,
        broken lines of ballads
        (her favourite's *He Was Glad*)
    or chattering little tunes
while she's busy loving.

Against the white dress Maria's skin seems darker.
    The dress fits perfectly around her,
        tightening at the thighs and breasts.
    Her dark shoulders curve and taper
    into her long dark neck.
Her dark almond eyes are charcoaled darker.

A sailor from Santander sent a torrent of kisses
    down Julie-Ann's back.
        He swore that Saint Magdalene's
        in holy Santander town
    could never hope to give
as much delight as he could give her kisses.

Eva de Lucia

People wonder if I'm slut or tinker,
    traveller, witch or crone,
        but nevertheless I'm here each year
        with a collapsible table and chair
    positioned in the sun
on Banbury Hill a week before Easter.

I am called Eva de Lucia,
    after my dear mother –
        a wonderful woman and mentor!
        She got me started. See my banner –
The Great Eva de Lucia –
Decoder-of-Dreams, Medium and Fortune-Teller.

I was fifteen when my mother died
    (it was a brain embolism)
        and I turned my head from home
        to work with death and dreams,
    just as my mother had done.
I know she's watching; she can see I've tried.

And many people come to Banbury Hill
    seeking out my wisdom.
        These folk come for their fortune,
        not to waste their time listening
    to gossip, tales and whispers
that I fly across the night in the shape of an owl!

I lie the cards down in a tidy manner,
    in rows or groups of four
        spread over the whole table.
        This is how I'm able
    to tell if you'll be rich or poor.
It's a power I inherited from my mother.

I read for a local man who frequently dreamed
    of the Old Cow's Bog
        and a woman, pretty and graceful
        standing there, with a silver halo
    hanging over her head.
A friend or lover wasn't all they seemed.

I know a girl who thought so much of her lover
    she wrote him a dozen letters
        after he died.
    She came to me and I advised
    not to let it worry her –
he'd read and cherished every letter.

Apples are always sadness and discontent.
    Anchors are trouble at home.
    These are not merely suggestions,
        but strict warnings and indications!
    We must heed our dreams
if we are to risk absolute fulfilment.

Snow's no good – it's a sign of sickness,
    but a snow-filled sky
        says you'll witness or arbitrate
        a bad and bitter argument.
    The first flakes are a man's lies,
but if seen as a blizzard, that means riches.

I could see a woman deftly weaving
    hoops of white heather
        with long strands of golden straw.
        She cut the pieces, loose and stray
    and drew it all together
with a blue ribbon. I knew she was dying.

Many men are sceptical of the cards,
    saying they bring problems
        and unwanted trouble
        to those who choose to meddle
    in such bunkum.
They mistake knowledgeable women for ignorant hags.

I've been called a bum and old fake,
    professional bullshitter,
        mistress of twaddle, drivel-driver,
        fraud, no-use huckster,
    swindler and ear-bender.
But at least I believe in what I say.

The Ghost

Not so much a spectre or phantom
as strand of thought that left a man
wondering how Cynthia's sequins and gimmicks,
all her shiny gewgaws
could take on light again
undeniably. A list of indisputable signs
proving Cynthia'd come back to town –
not least the paper roses strewing the floor
in front of the stage in the Pickle Bar.

Renowned for knowing every single dance,
every move and shake under the sun
and a repertoire of songs
she'd sing with a husky voice;
she could clear the bar with a stride.
It's not a rumour that this woman died
whilst dancing multiple jigs, spiels and reels
accompanied by a drunk man marking time
with a set of his dead mother's spoons.

Remember how she'd kick her stunning height,
her wobbling breasts came tumbling out
a feather-lined pink corset.
Now cuffs and ruffs and tights –
all that sparkling get-up's
locked inside a beaten-up box
under a chair in the Pickle Bar
where in her glory-days she used to dance
for a drink and a little applause.

Till now. In walked Cynthia fresh as a flower,
as if to complete the thousand and eight
revolutions of the *Dandy* (her favourite)
and we couldn't speak for fear.
As if she'd never died,
squat-footed and firm she stood
in a pink dress and high-heel shoes
at the front of the stage in the Pickle Bar
demanding silence, waving her arms in the air.

'When my corpse went winding through the streets,
stopping for a while here and there,
I couldn't help noticing, Lover,
where were you when the others wept?
It seems for all you care
you may as well've been screwing a lame whore
in an alley or shady corridor
while my corpse went winding by,
wrapped in a death-sheet, bound and dry.

How easily a man is led astray
when a woman sways her hips *that* way.
One thing that's for sure, Lover,
your cock's the well-known wanderer,
bolshy as a dog without a leash,
nosing for a bite up backstreets,
getting stuck inside loose sticky flaps,
the stinking slit of any willing floosie.
Let it never be said that you were choosy.

That I'd get mixed-up with someone like you.
But for all these curses I'm through
and your heart's a dish of ice.
Given less than half a chance
I bet you'd sell your sister
at some rough-edged Great Bazaar
for Consistent Love Rats and Liars –
trade her off for a foul-mouthed whore
who'd match you word for word, for a while.

Unheard, ignored or met with deaf-ears
and as far as shedding any tears –
spare me this humiliation,
when a dead honest woman
can get no rest,
when a woman's curses go unnoticed,
have less substance than gossip or ghost,
a little disturbed air or idle whisper
in the minds of those who matter, Lover.'

Love Rats

Bored with cards, chess or novel
    on a long afternoon?
        Lock all the doors,
          push back your hair and sleeves,
      lash on your apron,
try your hand at Love Rat Casserole!

Firstly take a good dose of love rats
    black to the bitter core –
        as many as you want
         or care to round up and count
    and soak for an hour
to soften up their foul exteriors.

Remove any black seeds, pips or stones
    also known as lies,
        shams, frauds, fibs and fiction,
        deceit and malicious-invention.
    These don't smell too nice –
scrub your hands after these vital extractions.

Now let's progress to the chopping-block –
    slam unwanted *extras*.
        Take hold of a sharp knife
        and squeezing tightly slice
    tongues, cocks and fingers –
leave nothing waggling, unfit for the pot.

Run a sharp blade over their backs
    right down to the bone –
        a good, clean, deep cut,
        then stuff the slits with coarse salt
    rubbed right in,
stuff the gobs with lumps of fat.

Now for the pièce-de-résistance, master flourish –
    a good strong stuffing
        of raspberries or radishes
        stuffed up their tight arses
    for a real tang!
A talking-point of any supper dish.

No need to bind the ankles and necks,
    but feel free to do so.
        A good length of twine or string
        stops them slipping and sloshing –
    and nice and tight now,
you're not taking grandma's dog for a walk.

Place the little buggers top-to-tail
    face down in a dish
        no less than choked on boozy gravy.
        They'll cook best that way –
    sweating the sticky stuff
from every little orifice and hole.

What you serve them with is up to you –
    anything from cabbage to cream
        and although the chef's no appetite
        (she really couldn't take a bite)
    she's wildly waving her spoon
to serve. Who wants a portion? Form a queue.

The Doll's House

Welcome to my second boudoir, my salon,
   my little beauty parlour
      La Petite Maison –
        you'll know it by the paper lantern
   hanging over the door
and its constant stream of gorgeous women.

Not one of the backstreets' *scalpel and slab.*
   My credentials are good,
      leaving you fresh and pampered –
      not mangled, crisped and toasted,
   broke and left for dead!
I only deal in butterflies and swans.

Give me, let's say, the most unsymmetrical woman –
   . I'll make her a Helen of Troy,
      turn a dog's slop-dinner
      into a red hot stunner
   in only half a day.
No hocus pocus – just the Art of Grooming.

I'm trained by a woman who only used her fingers,
   cloth and mirror – nothing more –
      no creams, colours or potions.
      I was hooked, got my own notions,
   took it from there.
Although successful she'd call me a swindler.

Mistress-Madeline of a thousand hairdos,
   the endless counter of creams,
      sticks, polish, soap and scents –
      just watch me turn cracked stumps
   into ruby red talons! –
coax life into a face as grey as mothballs.

I love a challenge and you're getting the best
   at rates that are reasonable.
      My grotto's very well equipped
      to handle any hag or misfit
   and I'll take control.
Trust my experience and impeccable taste.

I'm a devil-good hairdresser – curls or frizz,
    setting it straight or using a colour.
        What you don't want cut or plucked
        I'll coif into a masterpiece!
    I even do cunt-hair
and you should see my collection of antique wigs.

Sample my range of little special somethings
    for anyone and everyone –
        tried and tested treats and peps
        for tired eyes and thinning lips,
    wrinkles, crow's feet, sagging skin.
I'll razor out corns and cold cream bunions.

Throw out your arm, thigh or ankle
    for something more permanent –
        a dainty tattoo (fine ink
        or pig's blood needled under the skin)
    or what about a little ornament –
sparkling jewel to squeeze inside your navel!

Never less than seeking out perfection.
    Similar to an architect,
        ingenious creativity
        and steady hands are necessary.
    One false step
an angel's become a slop-faced slattern.

I swear the world's a sumptuous exhibition
    on a massive stage –
        piece of vaudeville or theatre,
        parade or brilliant gala
    with a stunning showcase
of a hundred thousand stunning women.

And I'm bored with the talk. Call it what you want –
    grease or war-paint,
        touch-up, non-essential,
        cover-up, superficial,
    a bunch of evils in the best arrangement –
it's all crap! Enhancing beauty's an art.

Lessons

1

This is not to tease you,
but teach your wandering hands
not to fumble with my breasts
as if looking for rabbits in bramble
or grabbing a shovel's handle.
Treat them more like goose eggs
new-laid, or running your palms
over simple flowers in June.

2

Watch how shadows move
and move your hands accordingly –
can you do it?
The way you tear at my clothes!
Do you want my chemise in threads
and marks all over my neck?
And not too forcefully –
now you're learning love.

3

Throw away the potions
you bought on Cuckoo Lane
and those love bracelets
from the old tinker.
A better, firmer lover
isn't based on such trinkets.
Handling the pace of love
isn't dealing with silly notions.

4

This is a worthy lesson.
Look how my thighs *flash*
in the noonday sun
filtering through the window.
By two they're cupped in shadow.
By eight the day is done
and darkness starts its own feast
of endless kissing and caressing.

5

Sometimes it's best to moderate.
It's right to be wary,
as with wine or cigarettes
or too much flesh, like a song
sickening when played too long.
It's easy to forget –
limits become hazy
while lost in a mire of enjoyment.

6

It's well worth noting
how bronze improves with time.
It's the same with love.
It was very touching
to see you brightly blushing
behind the outhouse.
But look how far we've come
from those first meetings.

7

Yes. Gifts are good,
but honest, little things
and not too lavish.
Don't smother with fancy buying –
perhaps hiding a shortcoming
or deficiency in some other place?
Ideal's a pair of earrings
to tease a lady's lobes.

8

I saw a single moment
when a man turned to fire
then stone, then fire again
and I knew him prone to hide
burning jealousies inside.
But why suffer such pain?
Why cheapen real desire
in a world of empty torment?

9

In India there are three sizes
of grown men and women.
But if you are too big,
penetrate softly,
not too forcefully
and not too deep, my God.
In this new way of loving
you're sure to find surprises.

10

A good recipe for love
is lavender (on the spray)
lemon (two sprigs)
subtle baby's breath,
almond-blossom (fresh –
not dried) mixed
and thrown generously
in a deep warm bath.

11

Not too serious or sloppy,
kissing's an art lost on many.
I'm sure you've heard of girls
practising on pillows –
shaping mouths in hollows
and holding their breath!
Well this is no girlish fancy –
come closer and let's play!

12

Love's a tidy gauge
of how faithful you are.
When you're telling tales
love's an idle matter –
or when looking over your shoulder
at other pretty girls
in the street or bar.
I think you get my message.

Couplet

What ho, Casanova! Tongue jammed with rust?
All your poems and love-spiels wriggling in the dust.

A Bestiary of Curses

Just like a precocious little piggy
   with a vanity case,
      you've stuck your snout too far
      and uprooted a nightmare –
   a perfect Pandora's Box –
everything tumbling out except Beauty.

Nothing's worse than the sound of your voice –
   impossible to put on,
      like some howling Bog Ass
      scratching his flea-eaten arse
   on a brake of thorns –
his howls your jarring voice. His arse your face.

You've as many manners as a scrapping cat –
   settling uneven scores
      in a makeshift boxing ring –
      the burst bellybutton,
   torn uterus and broken jaw.
What kind of monster settles like that?

Strained and puckered as a natterjack;
   the plume of bloody goo
      beating behind his sagging eyes
      or the stain where he'll die
   more agreeable than you –
chilly marrow in a plopping sack.

Like a magpie on a dung-heap,
   searching for something worth finding –
      pinching through each straw and seed,
      knee-deep in slop and mud.
   You can't eat jewels, darling.
This scene's as poor as you. Give it up.

That anaemic, scrubbed-out complexion
   isn't fooling anyone.
      A hen's got better legs than you –
      they're firmer and fatter too.
   Try a peck of food, skeleton.
Or hide that sallow face in the fly-ripe midden.

Where've you been hiding for so long –
   under stones with snakes?
      From the look on your pale face
      you *have* been in some dark place
   with things with crowds of legs.
Choose. Hell or Heaven? Where've you been?

Any number of monsters, demons, ghosts
   and other bloated nightmares
      climb and clamour to flee a mile,
      including the hangdog owl
   with eyes the size of saucers,
when they find you're passing through their haunts.

You'd lounge on some long-haired rug
   for a hundred years
      on the chance of a free snack
      with the patience of a saint.
   Patience? Bored to tears.
Do us a favour. Lie there till you're dead.

The Party

This place is full of ugly sisters
    and all their brothers too.
        But let's see who fares worst and best
        once I've put my eyes to the test.
    Crowd in and let's see!
Let's get the low-down on these jokers.

Melissa must be kept from the party platter.
    She pulls a brave face,
        but that doesn't stifle the rumour
        about her pubic hair
    crawling with fat lice.
I'll give her this – she's a model of composure.

Melinda's the crone whose been kept in a coffin
    for fifty long years.
        Get in close – look at her skin –
        watertight and paper-thin!
    Goodness – kill those lights
or she'll roast just like a little chicken!

Malcolm's nose is the dainty last morsel
    on a polished plate,
        his eyes bulge out his head
        like a pair of boiled eggs,
    and his baldy pate
polished bright as a shiny new whistle.

Stand well back! Don't get too close
    or you're going to get soaked!
        Why? Mellina drinks champagne
        like she's unblocking a drain,
    gargles it round her throat,
blasts it out her itchy little nose.

Watch out for Melosa's disgusting repertoire –
    putting on her free show –
        chasing the last cake crumb
        with the slug of her fat tongue
    round the dinner bowl,
or sucking off the fat pods of her fingers.

So who's the worst? Let me tell you.
Melona Goggle-Eyes.
From the most distended guts
to the fellow crashing his fists
around the champagne and pies,
Melona Goggle-Eyes. Worst on the menu.

Gossip

Not half as bad and far less vile
    to swallow a draught of arsenic
        or dose of poison
        from the devil's tongue
    than imbibe the bullshit
a mouthy gossiper is prone to peddle.

It's said Cherry's heart is made of sugar,
    being so sweet for boys and men
        and now she's sad and worn
        as the last sweet one
    took off quickly as he came.
Yes, yes. If you'll talk to a liar.

Trick

Here's the trick. There are a hundred tricks
if your brain's as slim as a toothpick.

Heard the one about the floating cannonball? –
that is, if you've heard anything at all.

You're so hoodwinked it's hard to bear;
I bet you'd call your eyes a pair of liars.

Ever wonder about those missing bracelets?
Take a peek between your neighbour's sheets.

But of course your little lover's so straight
she drinks her wine whilst hopping on one foot.

And of course she spins ten plates in the air
– *we believe you* – with the crook of her finger.

And yes it's true she did come home last night
(her mouth red-purple as a love-bite).

Yes; you seem quite tickled by Mistress Hoops;
hoops, that is, for you to jump through, Goose.

Don't mind if I leave before her final trick –
picking out her polished teeth with your prick.

Madam Aphrodisia

A cup of cocoa was never so much fun!
  But don't look so nervous –
      you too can act like Casanova!
    And I have all the answers!
  Or how six hundred women were serviced
by the one big appetite of an African king!

It's thought that caraway seeds assist digestion,
  but they're part of the lovers' cult
      so use them in your cooking!
    The bed-frame's furious rocking
  will be one result
and a lover who will humour any suggestion.

Three gull eggs from Mullingar
  neatly broken over
      a mixture of honey and ginger
      and spread on the cock of your lover
    should keep him loving deeper,
longer. Enjoy this little gift of pleasure.

A diet of fennel, lentils, peas and beans,
  washed down with a little wine
      will have you in top shape –
      you've never seen it stand so straight!
    And the strength of two men!
Mark how your delighted lady screams!

Forget the peacock tongues of ancient Rome.
  Try a single onion
      baked with butter and ginger
      and scrape of nutmeg for good measure.
    That's sure to get you going –
even Rome didn't know such hedonism!

The lands of hashish, strange roots and fasting –
  I have seen them all –
      China, India, Asia
      and know their importance to lovers
    who want to give their all.
Try cherries mixed with milk for lasting passion.

You have bought my wares, wise woman –
    the delicate white powder
        dusting your big tits
           will have him standing straight and stiff
    for hours on end, and longer!
Let nature work for you in rose and jasmine.

At one time Egyptian monks were bound
    never to eat fish.
        Perhaps it was just as well,
           as when members start to swell
    while partaking of Venus's gifts,
when would any sacred work get done?

A man who took a magpie's egg in the morning
    raw and on its own
        to boost his sexual prowess,
           said his wife was always late to dress.
    Yes. While he vomited in the pan!
Trust my wide knowledge and heed my warnings!

I've heard that rich women and men in China
    favour the musk of a deer –
        the gland under its tail
           pumped into a glass vial!
    It's a heavy price to bear –
costing as much as gold, frankincense or myrrh!

I have a special root, quite like ginseng,
    powerful, when mixed,
        so it's more of a personal recipe –
           but I warn you, use sparingly.
    There is nothing worse
than fading too soon from the heart of the action!

A ring of straw! An amulet of teeth!
    What good are they?
        You must beware of cranks
           spoiling love-play with pranks –
    but not my array –
they're sure to leave you joyful and out of breath!

The Bath

Annie closed her eyes and smelled shampoo.
    Thomas filled a chipped cup
        with warm clean water
        and using his fingers
    separated her hair at the top
in two and sent the water running through.

What was she thinking while he washed her hair –
    why was she smiling?
        She didn't say a word
        as smiling he worked
    his careful fingers on her skin
working at the temples, behind her ears

then up and round massaging everywhere
    till a generous thick froth
        had gathered there.
        He washed it all clear
    and with a soft-bristled brush
straightened out her hair and kissed her ear.

Her clean wet hair was carefully gathered,
    not leaving out any strand
        tight inside a towel.
        He poured a little oil
    into his cupped hand
which he warmed by rubbing his hands together

then mixed the oil with petals of jasmine,
    a pinch of potent lemon-seed,
        subtle candy-blossom
        and fine wheat-germ
    crushed so their scents released
on contact with her warm wet skin.

He rubbed the oily mixture over her shoulders,
    working his fingers and thumbs
        over her arms and back
        into the nape of her neck,
    the oil loosened by the steam
along her arms and inbetween her fingers.

Later Thomas unwrapped the towel
and her hair tumbled down,
long and wet and glossy
in a beautiful disarray
over her shoulders and arms
in a hundred ways, in waves and ripples

he gathered it up into his hands
as if her hair was being weighed
which he caressed and combed
carefully parted and wound
into a thick sleek braid
fastened by two little golden bands.

Tell Us

Tell us of the dazzling eyes
of folks who'd meet upon the Eve
for May Day's wild festivities
    and women known for changing.
Tell us of the raucous game
when raucous women chased the men
to sounds of fife and pipe and drum
    and women known for changing.

Tell us of pedlar and washerwoman –
him the fish and her the heron.
Fast as water, slick as semen
    she slipped him in like lightning.
She cracked him like a baby's skull,
played him like a little ball,
tossed him round just like a shell
    and slipped him in like lightning.

Tell us of the lawyer and whore –
him the mouse and her the hawk,
how she caught him by the throat
    and felt him there all throbbing.
She slipped her tongue where water flowed
and burrowed till she felt his blood
which beat and pulsed beneath her hand
    and felt him there all throbbing.

Tell us of the nun and friar –
her the fox and him the hare
going helter-skelter over the hill
    till he lay beneath her quivering.
How she climbed and crawled to play
astride his fat and furry belly
until she'd licked him clean and dry
    and he lay beneath her quivering.

Tell us of the jailor and thief –
him the hound and her the wolf,
how she'd suck and take his breath,
   his eyes all bright and dazzling.

How she'd prowl around his thighs,
squat on haunches, raise her blades,
run her tongue around her fangs,
   their eyes all bright and dazzling.

Tale

Here's a tale of silence.

I sat alone in a neat little room.
Here's a tale of silence.

I sat alone in a neat little room
on the Black Hill just before dawn.
Here's a tale of silence.

I sat alone in a neat little room
on the Black Hill just before dawn
when she came storming in.
Here's a tale of silence.

I sat alone in a neat little room
on the Black Hill just before dawn
when she came storming in,
while I sat stunned like a dead man.
Here's a tale of silence.

I sat alone in a neat little room
on the Black Hill just before dawn
when she came storming in,
while I sat stunned like a dead man
then lunged to hide my face in her dress.
Here's a tale of silence.

I sat alone in a neat little room
on the Black Hill just before dawn
when she came storming in,
while I sat stunned like a dead man
then lunged to hide my face in her dress
with her screaming *it's over Useless!*
Here's a tale of silence.

I sat alone in a neat little room
on the Black Hill just before dawn
when she came storming in,
while I sat stunned like a dead man
then lunged to hide my face in her dress
with her screaming *it's over Useless!*
and the pounding in my heart.
Here's a tale of silence.

I sat alone in a neat little room
on the Black Hill just before dawn
when she came storming in,
while I sat stunned like a dead man
then lunged to hide my face in her dress
with her screaming *it's over Useless!*
and the pounding in my heart
as I decided to throw in the lot.
Here's a tale of silence.

I sat alone in a neat little room
on the Black Hill just before dawn
when she came storming in,
while I sat stunned like a dead man
then lunged to hide my face in her dress
with her screaming *it's over Useless!*
and the pounding in my heart,
as I decided to throw in the lot,
rubbing the nub of ice behind my eyes.
Here's a tale of silence.

I sat alone in a neat little room
on the Black Hill just before dawn
when she came storming in,
while I sat stunned like a dead man
then lunged to hide my face in her dress
with her screaming *it's over Useless!*
and the pounding in my heart,
as I decided to throw in the lot,
rubbing the nub of ice behind my eyes
and her saying *look what you've done to us.*
Here's a tale of silence.

Booley's Boys Tell All

We don't know much, but we know what we saw:
ten men wandering over Gravyclaw,
with heads bowed and cassocks tied with twine.
They passed old Gillies' byre in single file,
walked the Mallow Road and climbed the stile,
stable as bends in branches, stones in rain.

Uncle Hughie said to watch their faces,
mostly hidden by the robes, but flashes
could be glimpsed and they were white as stone
and cold from greeting every cold-cracked dawn
this world has sent. And these men slept on stone,
were lightly fed on bread and sweetened water,
said their prayers in chant and hymn and psalter
and washed themselves in every stony dawn.

Have You Heard

Have you heard how the wars began?
   It's a tale you should hear.
Have you heard how the wars began?
   If you'll lend an ear
I'll tell you how the awful wars began.

Never did a man go so mad for a woman.
   She was sweet as honey.
She made his head throb like an old melon –
   he was *that* crazy!
If she said *kill a man* he'd shoot that person.

Well, this cutthroat liked to move his hand
   around her skin of silk,
making sure it tingled, wept and bled
   diamonds (or so he said).
He liked to make her chatter like a bird.

Flouncy, bouncy girls with a whoop and call
   tangoed in a hall
while this devil screwed his squirming girl,
   her cunt a bed of coals.
He wanted to make the moon rattle and fall.

He rode her like a horse across the sheets,
   pulled her by the hair,
used his hands as silver bridle bits,
   pushed her mouth to water.
He loved to keep her firmly in her wits.

One time he pushed and thrust so hard
   she clawed him in the face.
He loved it. He was so mad
   he could throw a knife!
And later while he slept she tiptoed out.

And that is how the wars began.
   Have you heard a tale like that before?
That is how the wars began.
   Was it worth lending your ear?
That is how the awful wars began.

Letter to Patty

I write to tell you that I'm better,
or well enough to write another letter.
I'm very sorry it's been a while,
I've been through, well, a black spell,
a 'freezing' of the brain.
I'm in the care of a Doctor Matthew Horn –
originally an apothecary from York, a good man
you'll be glad, I'm sure, to hear.
Yes. I'm really feeling better, brighter.

I'm strictly heeding Doctor Horn's suggestions
for a gentle, gradual recuperation,
dealing with life after paralysis –
eased by gentle walks in Riddle Forest
and cold deep baths.
Riddle Hall has two other buildings –
Laws and White Fells and tea gardens,
orangery and large duck pond.
Yes. You were right. This isn't so bad.

What's more luxurious than waking at eight
with the light and an hour to meditate
before the rattling breakfast trolley.
I'm relearning a little Natural History.
I already know Wood Sage,
Green Hellebore and Black Bryony.
We had snow on New Year's Day.
I've also started writing a little poetry
which I like to do beneath the elm trees.

At nine o'clock sharp you'd meet our Captain –
lost in the brouhaha of a great wind,
straddling his iron bed
and sailing a ship through a storm,
roaring from the prow (the bed)
The Duchess! The Duchess! Men! To starboard side!
while thrashing himself from side to side,
wincing through an icy, freezing shower.
Indeed, this show can sometimes play for hours.

His yells can carry through from room to room,
past the sleepwalkers and the ghosts,
the woman with the photographs,
past the sweeper who finishes then starts again,
sweeping from room to room,
past the white-faced men like children
standing in a crooked-straight line
like a row of bottles on a shelf
playing cards or talking to themselves.

How are all my darling little boys?
Just last night I had a dream –
it was nothing, about little William,
and Frederick – how are his studies?
My mind is quite empty.
In fact nothing bothers me.
I'm sure you'd agree this is a pleasant country.
Spring will soon be coming in,
which, I'm sure you'd agree, is a good thing.

Yes. I'm really feeling much better.
Doctor Horn promises a full recovery.
I hope you're keeping well, Patty,
and now you have another letter!
I really can't complain,
really, these past few years I've felt fine.
I wonder when we'll meet again?
Send my love and kisses to the children,
I am my dear your affectionate husband John.

Hunger

It's true that hunger's sharper than a thorn.
    Meet the Loneliest Man in the World –
        he's been reading books for years
        yet still he's full of tears,
    his only friend
the curds and syrups of his brain.

It's true that he's been dreaming of your hand
    combing through his hair
        and your laugh as light as a feather
        (it's true it makes men stagger
    into the gutter, but no matter!)
Make way for the Happiest Man in the World!

Mrs Jones, Whilst Dying

They say when Mrs Jones lay dying
she insisted on having the whitest sheets
and transparent cuts of delicate meats,
drops of cream and honey and wine
dropped on her lips. She said to feast
one only needed to taste and then determine
the depth of the body and its blood.
She said to ravish on rumps of toughened meat,
lumps of bread and gruel as thick as mud,
washed down with wine as strong as sweat,
killed all kindness in a woman's soul.
Why would spirits ever settle there? –
within another gruel-soaked fool,
when the soul must be dainty and light as air.

Wimple Fair

Who hasn't been to Wimple Fair,
    or waited for that time of year
        during long days
        of melancholy
    when the Fair comes to town.
Deny it's the best time of the year.

Look how a man on stilts freely walks
    between *Night of the Premonitions,*
        Mind Clarities,
        Sugar Pastries,
    Sweet-Dream Definitions
and numerous other high-coloured tents.

Watch the painted man who juggles fire
    then thrusts the fire into his throat,
        coughs and spits out smoke –
        (women love this bit)
    then takes a little drink
while women laugh and scream for more.

Near the water-tents the noise gets louder
    where vats and pans and sinks
        hold more beer and wine
        than ten fat men
    could possibly drink
over the longest, driest summer.

There's plenty to eat. Visit *Rattling Hives*
    for apples boiled in a jam-sloshed barrel,
        skewered on sticks
        or next to the *Tent-of-Poets*
there's cakes and bread-twists
and Meg Beanie's famous cold pies.

Don't dare miss the puzzle-breakers –
    the world's codes and enigmas,
        all its mysteries
        their very specialty!
    For the price of a shot or beer
ask them anything, they'll give you an answer.

Of course there's dancers and music-makers –
   plenty of these, dozens and dozens
       playing shakers and harps,
       bells and zithers and flutes
   from sun-up to sun-down
when darkness makes them play even louder!

No matter how close you watch the necklace-spinners
   spinning endless lengths of threads
       you'll always see
       light embroidery
   falling from their hands
and never understand the craft of their fingers.

Take a little time to sit and wonder
   on the work of the dream-makers
       hidden in their tent
       and totally intent
   on making bystanders marvel
on miracles so light and full of pleasure.

Remember you placed petals inside your cunt
   and river-clay under your tongue,
       snorted powdered mallow.
       Revisit Mrs Wimple,
   find out what needs to be done.
It's her wish you dream whatever you want.

Three Songs

And every year he celebrated spring
    by opening a bottle of wine,
filling a wide cup to the brim
    and singing *Catch-the-Plack*
till his lungs ached
    and his head was like a bobbing cork.

In the lit dark rooms of Molly's place
    in lipstick and green dress,
the accordion hugged loose to her chest
    she played a round of songs
for the birthday of Maisie Brown;
    Sailor, Polish these Toes of Mine.

At *Send-Offs* you'll find a man in a nook,
    looking like a tattered coat
hung over a beaten stick,
    tapping out a ballad or song
to keep his heart warm
    as was his custom and no one stopped him.

Drinking Song

Sung with gusto at the Pinweary Arms

Amber glory and golden gulp
    Or Bacchus' brainless twist;
A shot of death or bullet's breath,
    Under the table pissed.

Belly belch, a skin of sack
    And grains of grime and toil;
Pudding's plotter, rider's rack
    And brainless brains all spoiled.

Music's chanter, most-men's banter,
    Twirl and furl and down;
Baited hook and line and sinker,
    Seed and sun and flame.

Degree, disgrace, digestive,
    John Barleycorn and bread;
The crumpled cockle's corrective,
    The years, the tears, the dead.

Men in Love

She'd sit telling stories all morning
   on a chair by the bar
      to a widening crowd
      gathered round
    while smoking a long cigar;
talked about women, the trouble they bring.

'Nothing lasts for long that's calm or peaceful.
   I've known many men
     who wanted an easy life
     unspoiled by love,
   who slept in their beds for years alone
and liked it that way, uncomplicated and single.

Then the charms or a woman came their way.
   Suddenly they got no sleep,
     lost all wit,
     forgot to eat,
    were wracked by want,
their mellow hours replaced with mindless worry.

I do not lie! A thousand anxieties
   gathered where there was none.
     This is the condition
     the allure of a woman
   can force on an unassuming man.
Trust me, there are plenty of stories!

A young man – this is no lie I'm telling –
   waited by an ex-lover's door
     for three long days.
     She laughed in his face
   when she finally unlocked the door
to let his rival in.

Or the man who spent his entire fortune
   on a low-life whore
     who'd caught his eye
     in a shady dive.
   He lost his fortune and more
in the hope he'd found the perfect woman.

Or the man who'd fallen in love again –
   thirteen times that week!
      As you can imagine
      all this female toying
   left him a terrible wreck –
a sorry joke enjoyed by vicious women.

Watch out for a lightly crinkled brow.
   Don't fall for a tantrum,
      a mess of tears,
         soft words in your ear –
   all delivered with measured cunning
and assuring her part in your downfall.

No doubt she'll love to play nasty little games
   with your delicate mind,
      all her idle play
      leaving you half-crazy
   wondering what you did this time –
all part of her sly and devious plan!

So men! There are many who've been burned.
   Pull close the shutters
      of your little hearts.
      Give women no part
   in your life and its personal matters.
Don't deny this lesson. You were warned!'

Women in Love

Ladies. We're all prone to falling in love
    but you must beware of men.
        They're unwanted trouble,
        more like arch rivals
    no matter how charming or handsome –
all weaponry they're not scared to use.

View love as a type of tournament
    filled with plots and stratagems –
        not having relations,
        but a competition
    in will power and mind-games –
each the other's staunch opponent.

Trouble can always be found in a man's eyes.
    Ladies beware! He's very sly,
        sneakily ranging,
        drifting and roving
    lecherous peepers over women nearby
and then he'll say he loves you – pure lies!

Watch out for those with a deep suspicion.
    Invite a male friend to chat
        and now he trusts no one,
        loathes anyone
    you so much as look at
and calls this a show of his affection!

When you find your patience is running thin
    because he's acted up again,
        alarmed by jealousy
        say he's temporary
    and undergoing a test-run,
merely a warm-up, an audition!

A man's a mire of puzzles and uncertainties –
    riddled with silences and secrets
        and the stolid intention
        of keeping them
    tight against his stubborn chest
while your exhausted from probing these mysteries.

Nothing's more boring than a man's boasting
    about his strength or virility,
        acting the Great Lover
        when his only power
    is his startling ability
in repeated half-arsed attempts and snoring!

No doubt he'll try to abuse your trust.
    He'll probably be a bad liar,
        but that won't stop him
        biting his malicious tongue
    and telling plenty more.
Avoid this disgusting behaviour at all cost.

He'll never be able to keep his hands still –
    his notion of tenderness
        manhandling your breasts,
        pawing at thighs and legs.
    He's oblivious of kindness,
only knowing how to grab or maul.

Now ladies – you must heed this lesson.
    In the event you fall for a man
        and your heart's burning
        stuff it with my warning,
    that should quell the pain.
Trust me! I'm an experienced woman!

The Other Teller

A Tale from Jimmy Currie

One time we listened to him tell
    a tale each night for ten nights
        at the pub in the village.
    They lasted for ages –
    wrapping-up at half-light,
commencing with the breakfast-bell.

Once he'd danced on a table with a queen,
    in royal feasting halls,
        wrote his phone number
        on her glass slipper
    (she'd asked him for the details)
using her coral lipstick as a pen.

He'd wrestled with fifty men and women –
    a group of chefs and waiters,
        cleaners and dishwashers,
        cutlery polishers
    for an imaginary wager,
finally losing to a lady who folded linen.

Open-eyed he'd watched a mad woman
    consume a vial of poison –
        she'd finished it
        inside a minute
    (it could kill a hundred men)
then dance a jig on her husband's coffin.

As well as telling tales he loved to sing.
    Once he'd banded together
        in a male chorus
        with friends Spud and Haggis,
    Hum and Dick Dinger,
performing for groups of lonely women.

He'd seen a blind man rifling through
    an old case of bric-à-brac
        searching for his drum
        having promised a song
    to his dead sweetheart.
He found it dust-covered, good as new.

A mother strewed a bed with blossom and glitter,
    laid out her daughter's dress,
        tied a knot of nettles,
        bread and bluebells
    against newly-weds' secrets,
knew nothing of the knife in her daughter's slipper.

The crowd was silenced. He wiped his brow,
    resumed the story of the man
        shot in the belly
        who rode off wildly
    on a black horse, waving his hand
in the air in the ultimate ghost-show.

Maybe a tale-teller, but never a liar.
    He could look so utterly grave,
        deadpan, unflappable
        then suddenly sparkle,
    tears rolling down his face
like when he told the tale of the brassière!

Waving off loud applause he sniffed,
    recounted the long drive
        (a thousand flat kilometres)
        with a hitchhiker
    from Bitter Loans to Hives
by telling the story of another man's life.

His stories were sensitive and ridiculous,
    passionate and outrageous –
        he was the best poet
        beyond all doubt,
    leaving crowds incredulous,
completely awestruck and a little suspicious.

The Dark Queen
A Second Tale from Jimmy Currie

The juice had been extracted from lime and laurel.
    Lilies had been gathered
        crushed and dipped
            in salt and cow-dung
        moulded and turned
            around a long wick
    and carefully lighted –
inviting a man to dream whatever he will!

I dreamed of absolute beauty – the Dark Queen
    overpowered me with her charms –
        her dark, smooth skin,
            the bracelets on her arms,
        like shaking stacks of spume,
            stones that shone like moons,
    no less than hypnotising a man.
But this was more than trickery or dream.

There are men who spend their entire lives
    following the Alicanto –
        a beautiful and majestic bird
            famed for spending time
        hunting for beautiful gems,
            teasing jewels from rock,
    separating precious metal
from stone and haunting men's greedy dreams.

Late at night at a place called Straitson Falls
    by the edge of reedy bogs
        or calm stream waters
            where Alicanto are wading
        men are quietly watching,
            waiting to move forward,
    force the bird into a burlap bag
whilst tightly squeezing the neck so its call's

stuck inside its reed-thin throat.
But it's the bird's great belly
and what can be found therein
that really matters.
Knifing past feathers,
bird-flesh and bone
gold and splinters of emeralds and rubies
and once a two-ounce heavy golden brooch

have all been found lying in its gut,
like a secret Aladdin's den,
housing a hoard of gems –
diamond chunks and droplets,
well-wrought bracelets,
finer than any craftsman's –
one of which can be seen
dancing on the Dark Queen's wrist.

She was wearing a long cape, or cloak
or perhaps it was more like a loose mantle,
but certainly not a dress
and it fell from her shoulder
clearly exposing her
beautiful left breast,
its glorious erect nipple
and she didn't even move it back.

Cut close to the skin her glorious hair
was meticulously hennaed
using the finest pods
and her strong scalp
rubbed with buttermilk
and some potent herbs
making the smell of fresh orchids
seem stale. There were jewels in her ears.

She sported big stones that were beautiful and black,
fat and fine and rich ones –
the world's finest onyx
dancing on her dark skin,
shaking and running
up and down her arms –
and others with white veins,
lush with streaks of salamander's fat!

Pressed out of the sticky gizzard
    of a newly-slaughtered cock,
        the beautiful stone –
            clear alectoria
        imbued her
            with power over a man.
The stone hung around her neck
and bounced on her breasts. I was bothered;

if I were to go to bed with this beautiful woman
    and really taste her kiss
        it'd be covers of cold silk
            in a temperate room;
        her fingers would be warm,
            her face and lips
    smeared with lipstick,
herb-scents bursting as I held her down –

I watched her feet pound the ground and dance –
    bare feet smoothed with oil,
        ankles decorated
            with strings of swallow-stones,
        red and tied in rings.
            Her toenails were brightly painted
    with smears of ochre and cochineal
as she held her arms in the air as if in a trance

her eyes were closed, her neck arched like a swan's
    held up then dropped with the drum
        she danced to the pounding beat.
        All I could do was watch
    this furious beautiful dance
        where oil turned to sweat
    streaking her brow, enrapturing a man
who wondered if he figured in her dreams.

The Drowned Man

A Third Tale from Jimmy Currie

Serious for ritual the May Dippers
    formed a neat procession
        to breast the freezing waters
           for May Day –
        more like shivering babies
           than strong-hearted swimmers –
the twenty-or-so men and women
who waded in to bravely take the waters.

Their lines fanned out like chains of bunting
    broken up by the water's pushing.
    It was then a bather
        found a man's body
    floating harmlessly
        in an inlet of quiet water.
The twenty-or-so stopped bathing
and quietly, solemnly brought the body in.

              *

A bloated wallet flapped out his pocket
    onto the floor. It was thrown away
        water-wrecked and empty.
        Salt matted his clothes
        and the sea had swallowed his shoes
        evidently.
    There were also twenty
or thirty sand-dollars and an old bus ticket.

Sixteen women worked tirelessly
    around the drowned man's body,
        soaking clothes with gin,
           lifting tongues and lashes
    of sea reeds and grasses
        that had washed around him,
    wiping the salt from his skin
and the brooch of barnacles on his left thigh.

They cut off the remains of a shirt,
  peeled it from his broad back,
    shook out cockle shells
      from ramshackle trousers,
    splayed his long fingers
      to cut his bone-white nails,
  removed a rusty chain from his neck
and a salt-eaten watch from his wrist.

A heavy pitcher of haw-flavoured oil
  silently passed amongst the women.
    The oil was fed into his fingers,
      rubbed over his legs,
    feet and hands and loins,
      buttocks, neck and shoulders,
  chest and belly, back and arms,
the little white scar on his left ankle.

And they couldn't help noticing
  as they took a bright new blade
    over his prickly chin
      the look in his eyes –
    calm and dissatisfied,
      or was it unconcern,
  or was he endlessly bored,
letting his eyes stare past the lot of them?

His hair was as black as a glossy blackbird
  entangled in a net of weed
    and it was a glory-box.
      Mary'd found a coin,
    Irma a little gem
      red as the tail of a fox
  tucked behind his ear
and two pearls as well 's a handful of sand.

But that was nothing. Katie found
  a beautiful black mantle
    embroidered with bright colours,
      a fan of white feathers,
    bundle of love letters
      dedicated to the reader,
  a *behold-the beauty* mirror
and *you-choose-the-miracle* charm.

Nora knew he was a treasure trove.
She pushed passed sand and seaweed,
mountains of broken coral,
met a top-hatted man
who ushered her in
through a satin curtain,
into a white-gold gig,
closed the door and told the horses to move.

Ballad of the Lovers

The wind is working out a hollow patch.
My lover raised his arm to fasten the catch,
battened down the hatch and sparked a match.

Listen to the wind pressing the catch.
Whipping the flame, bat-batting the hatch.
The wind is trying to hollow out a patch!